The Ultimate Beef

Stew Cookbook

The Best of The Homemade Beef Stew
Recipes

BY: Valeria Ray

License Notes

A Special Reward for Purchasing My Book!

Thank you, cherished reader, for purchasing my book and taking the time to read it. As a special reward for your decision, I would like to offer a gift of free and discounted books directly to your inbox. All you need to do is fill in the box below with your email address and name to start getting amazing offers in the comfort of your own home. You will never miss an offer because a reminder will be sent to you. Never miss a deal and get great deals without having to leave the house! Subscribe now and start saving!

https://valeria-ray.gr8.com

Contents

Homemade Beef Stew Recipes 6

(1) Classic Beef Stew 7

(2) Italian Beef Stew 11

(3) Slow Cooker Beef and Vegetable Stew 14

(4) Crockpot Beef Stew 17

(5) Homemade Beef and Lentil Soup 20

(6) Red Wine Beef Stew 23

(7) Beef Stout Stew 26

(8) Cuban Beef Stew 30

(9) Classic Homemade Beef Stew 33

(10) Slow Cooker Beef Tip Stew with Rice 37

(11) Irish Coffee Beef Stew 39

(12) Wild Mushroom Beef Stew 43

(13) Slow Cooker Beef Bourguignon Stew 46

(14) Mexican Beef Stew 49

(15) Beef Stew Pot Pie 52

(16) Guinness Beef Stew with Cheddar Herb Dumplings 56

(17) Instant Pot Beef Stew 60

(18) Beef Stew Shepherd's Pie 63

(19) French Beef Stew 66

(20) Irish Beef Stew 69

(21) Beef Stew Burgundy 73

(22) Fall Beef Stew 76

(23) Old Fashioned Beef Stew 80

(24) Chunky Beef Stew 83

(25) Hearty Beef Stew 86

About the Author 90

Author's Afterthoughts 92

Homemade Beef Stew Recipes

MMMMMMMMMMMMMMMMMMMMMMMMMMMMMMMMMMMMM

(1) Classic Beef Stew

This is a classic beef stew that will warm up every part of your body with practically every bite. The fat from the beef melts as it cooks, tenderizing the beef even more.

Yield: 8 servings

Cooking Time: 2 hours and 30 minutes

List of Ingredients:

- ¼ cup of all-purpose flour
- ½ teaspoons of salt
- ¼ teaspoons of black pepper
- 2 pounds of beef roast, cut into cubes
- 3 Tablespoons of butter
- 1 tablespoon of vegetable oil
- 2 ribs of celery, chopped
- 1 onion, chopped
- 2 Tablespoons of tomato paste
- ½ cup of dried red wine
- 1 pound of white potatoes, cut into quarters
- 3 carrots, cut into chunks
- 10 sprigs of thyme
- 6 sprigs of parsley
- 2 bay leaves
- 3 cups of low sodium beef broth
- ½ teaspoons of Worcestershire sauce
- ¾ cups of pickled onions, drained
- ¾ cup of peas

MMMMMMMMMMMMMMMMMMMMMMMMMMMMMMMMMMMM

Methods:

1. In a bowl, add in the all-purpose flour, dash of salt and black pepper. Stir well to mix. Add in the beef cubes. Toss well to coat.

2. In a Dutch oven set over medium heat, add in 2 tablespoons of butter and the vegetable oil. Add in the beef cubes. Cook for 20 minutes or until browned. Transfer onto a plate and set aside.

3. Add in the remaining butter into the Dutch oven. Add in the chopped celery and chopped onion. Cook for 5 minutes or until soft. Add in the tomato paste. Continue to cook for 2 minutes.

4. Add in the dried red wine. Deglaze the bottom of the Dutch oven. Cook for 2 minutes.

5. Add the beef cubes back into the Dutch oven. Add in the white potato quarters, chopped carrots, sprigs of thyme, sprigs of parsley and bay leaves. Stir gently to mix. Add in the low sodium beef broth and Worcestershire sauce. Allow to come to a boil.

6. Cover and place into the oven to bake for 45 minutes at 350 degrees.

7. Add in the pickled onions. Cover and continue to bake for an additional 15 minutes. Remove the cover and continue to cook for 30 to 40 minutes or until the beef and vegetables are soft.

8. Add in the peas. Continue to bake for 5 minutes.

9. Remove and set aside to cool for 10 minutes.

10. Serve with a garnish of chopped parsley.

(2) Italian Beef Stew

This is the perfect beef stew to make if you are craving the flavor of authentic Italian cuisine. It is so delicious, even the pickiest of eaters won't be able to resist this dish.

Yield: 4 to 6 servings

Cooking Time: 5 hours and 15 minutes

List of Ingredients:

- ¾ cup of all-purpose flour
- 2 Tablespoons of powdered garlic
- Dash of salt and black pepper
- 1 ½ pounds of beef chuck roast, trimmed and chopped into 1 ½ inch sized cubes
- Extra virgin olive oil, as needed
- 1 red onion, chopped
- 6 cloves of garlic, chopped
- 4 to 5 rainbow carrots, chopped
- 1 cup of dried red wine
- 2 cups of vegetable broth
- 1, 28 ounce can of tomato, peeled and whole
- 4 to 5 sprigs of thyme
- 2 sprigs of rosemary
- 16 ounces of cremini mushrooms, thinly sliced

MMMMMMMMMMMMMMMMMMMMMMMMMMMMMMMMMMMM

Methods:

1. In a bowl, add in the all-purpose flour and powdered garlic. Stir well to mix.

2. Pat dry the beef cubes with a few paper towels. Season the beef with a dash of salt and black pepper. Add into the bowl with the flour mix. Toss well until coated.

3. In a cast iron skillet set over medium to high heat, add in 2 tablespoons of olive oil. Add in the beef cubes. Cook for 5 minutes or until browned. Transfer the beef into the bowl of a slow cooker.

4. Add in the remaining ingredients into the slow cooker except for the sliced mushrooms. Stir well to mix.

5. Cover and cook on the highest setting for 4 hours and 30 minutes.

6. Add in the sliced mushrooms. Cover and cook for an additional 30 minutes.

7. Serve immediately.

(3) Slow Cooker Beef and Vegetable Stew

This is a delicious and savory dish I know you will want to constantly come home to. Add a dash of parmesan cheese to each serving for the tastiest results.

Yield: 8 servings

Cooking Time: 6 hours and 50 minutes

List of Ingredients:

- 1 ½ pounds of beef chuck roast, cut into cubes
- 3 potatoes, peeled and cut into cubes
- 3 cups of water
- 1 ½ cups of baby carrots
- 1, 10.75 ounce can of condensed tomato soup
- 1 onion, chopped
- 1 rib of celery, chopped
- 2 Tablespoons of Worcestershire sauce
- 1 tablespoon of browning sauce
- 2 teaspoons of beef bouillon granules
- 1 clove of garlic, minced
- 1 teaspoon of white sugar
- ¾ teaspoons of salt
- Dash of black pepper
- ¼ cup of cornstarch
- ¾ cup of cold water
- 2 cups of peas

MMMMMMMMMMMMMMMMMMMMMMMMMMMMMMMMMMMM

Methods:

1. In a large slow cooker, add in the beef chuck roast cubes, water, potato cubes, baby carrots, chopped onion, can of condensed tomato soup, Worcestershire sauce, chopped celery, browning sauce, beef bouillon granules, minced garlic and white sugar. Season with a dash of salt and black pepper. Stir gently to mix.

2. Cover and cook on the lowest setting for 6 to 8 hours or until the beef is soft.

3. In a bowl, add in the cornstarch and water. Whisk until smooth in consistency. Pour into the stew and stir well to incorporate.

4. Add in the peas.

5. Cover and continue to cook on the highest setting for 30 minutes or until thick in consistency.

6. Serve immediately.

(4) Crockpot Beef Stew

This is a hearty and savory beef stew that is perfect to make during those long and cold winter nights. Loaded with plenty of beef, this beef stew will leave you feeling full for hours.

Yield: 8 servings

Cooking Time: 10 hours and 20 minutes

List of Ingredients:

- 3 pounds of beef fat, trimmed and cut into cubes
- ¼ cup of all-purpose flour
- 1 tablespoon of extra virgin olive oil
- 4 cups of beef broth
- 1 teaspoon of Worcestershire sauce
- 3 Tablespoons of tomato paste
- ½ teaspoons of salt
- ¼ teaspoons of black pepper
- 1 tablespoon of smoked paprika
- 1 teaspoon of ground cumin
- 1 tablespoon of dried oregano
- 1 onion, chopped
- 5 cloves of garlic, minced
- 6 potatoes, peeled and cut into cubes
- 2 carrots, peeled and thinly sliced
- 1 cup of green beans, ends trimmed and cut in half

MMMMMMMMMMMMMMMMMMMMMMMMMMMMMMMMMMMMMM

Methods:

1. In a Ziploc bag, add in the beef cubes and all-purpose flour. Seal the bag and shake to coat.

2. In a skillet set over medium to high heat, add in the olive oil. Add in the beef. Cook for 8 to 10 minutes or until browned.

3. Add in the beef broth and deglaze the bottom of the skillet. Add in the Worcestershire sauce, tomato paste, smoked paprika, ground cumin and dried oregano. Season with a dash of salt and black pepper. Stir well to mix. Allow to come to a boil. Remove from heat.

4. Add in the chopped onion, minced garlic, potatoes cubes, sliced carrots and sliced green beans. Stir well to mix. Pour into a crockpot.

5. Cover and cook on the lowest setting for 8 to 10 hours or on the highest setting for 5 to 6 hours.

6. Serve with a garnish of chopped parsley.

(5) Homemade Beef and Lentil Soup

This is a dish that will warm both your body and your belly. It is perfect to make any night of the week when you need to spoil yourself.

Yield: 8 servings

Cooking Time: 1 hour and 40 minutes

List of Ingredients:

- 2 Tablespoons of extra virgin olive oil
- 2 ½ pounds of beef chuck roast, cut into 1 inch sized cubes
- 1 onion, chopped
- 3 cloves of garlic, minced
- 4 carrots, thinly sliced
- 3 stalks of celery, thinly sliced
- 1 ½ cup of dried green lentils
- 1, 28 ounce can of tomatoes, crushed
- 6 cups of beef stock
- 1 cup of dried red wine
- 3 bay leaves
- 1 tablespoon of dried thyme
- Dash of cayenne pepper
- 3 Tablespoons of tarragon, chopped
- Dash of salt and black pepper

MMMMMMMMMMMMMMMMMMMMMMMMMMMMMMMMMMMM

Methods:

In a pot set over medium to high heat, add in the olive oil. Add in the onions. Cook for 5 minutes or until soft.

Add in the beef chuck cubes and minced garlic. Stir well to mix. Continue to cook for 5 to 10 minutes or until the beef is browned.

Add in the sliced carrots, sliced celery, dried green lentils, crushed tomatoes, beef stock, dried red wine, bay leaves, dried thyme and cayenne pepper. Season with a dash of salt and black pepper. Stir well to mix. Allow to come to a boil. Lower the heat to low. Cover and cook for 45 minutes to 1 hour or until the lentils are soft.

Add in the chopped tarragon. Stir well to incorporate. Remove from heat and serve immediately.

(6) Red Wine Beef Stew

This is an inexpensive beef stew you can make whenever you need to make dinner on a budget. Best of all, it makes so much you will have leftovers for a few days.

Yield: 4 to 6 servings

Cooking Time: 2 hours and 30 minutes

List of Ingredients:

- 2 Tablespoons of butter, soft
- 2 onions, sliced into rings
- 6 cloves of garlic, cut into halves
- 3 Tablespoons of all-purpose flour
- 2 pounds of beef shirt steaks, cut into pieces
- 2 Tablespoons of extra virgin olive oil
- 3 bay leaves
- 1 ½ cups of dried red wine
- 1 tablespoon of pureed tomato
- 1 ¼ cup of beef stock
- 1 cup of mushrooms, sliced into halves
- Parsley, chopped and for garnish

MMMMMMMMMMMMMMMMMMMMMMMMMMMMMMMMMMM

Methods:

1. Preheat the oven to 300 degrees.

2. In a Dutch oven set over medium to high heat, add in the butter. Add in the onions. Cook for 10 minutes or until the onions turn brown. Transfer into a bowl and set aside.

3. In a Ziploc bag, add in the all-purpose flour, dash of black pepper and salt. Stir gently to mix. Add in the beef pieces and seal the bag. Shake vigorously to coat.

4. In the Dutch oven, add in the olive oil. Add in the beef pieces and bay leaves. Cook for 2 to 3 minutes or until browned.

5. Pour in the dried red wine and deglaze the bottom of the Dutch oven. Add the cooked onion mix back into the Dutch oven. Add in the pureed tomato and beef stock. Allow to come to a simmer. Cover and transfer into the oven. Bake for 1 hour.

6. Add in the sliced mushroom halves. Place back into the oven to bake for an additional 30 minutes.

7. Remove and serve with a topping of chopped parsley.

(7) Beef Stout Stew

This is a delicious beef stew that every adult in your household will fall in love with. Be sure to serve with freshly baked bread for the tastiest results.

Yield: 8 servings

Cooking Time: 2 hours and 30 minutes

List of Ingredients:

- 2 pounds of chuck roast, boneless and cut into cubes
- Dash of salt and black pepper
- 3 Tablespoons of canola oil, evenly divided
- ¼ cup of all-purpose flour
- 1 onion, chopped
- 12 ounces of stout beer, evenly divided
- 4 cloves of garlic, minced
- 1, 6 ounce can of tomato paste
- 1 tablespoon of Worcestershire sauce
- 1 tablespoon of white sugar
- 1 tablespoon of dried thyme
- 1 teaspoon of white pepper
- 2 bay leaves
- 2, 32 ounce container of beef stock
- 5 Yukon gold potatoes, chopped
- 5 carrots, chopped
- 4 stalks of celery, chopped

MMMMMMMMMMMMMMMMMMMMMMMMMMMMMMMMMMMM

Methods:

1. In a Dutch oven set over medium to high heat, add in 2 tablespoons of canola oil.
2. Pat the beef cubes dry with a few paper towels. Transfer into a bowl. Season with a dash of salt and black pepper. Add in ¼ cup of all-purpose flour. Toss well until coated.
3. Transfer the coated beef cubes into the Dutch oven. Cook for 5 minutes or until browned on all sides. Transfer into a bowl and set aside.
4. Add in 1 tablespoon of canola oil. Add in the onion. Cook for 5 minutes or until soft.
5. Add in the stout beer and deglaze the bottom of the Dutch oven. Add in the tomato paste, minced garlic, white sugar, Worcestershire sauce, dried thyme, dash of white pepper and bay leaves. Stir well to mix. Allow to come to a boil. Lower the heat to low.
6. Add in the cooked beef. Allow to come to a boil. Lower the heat to low. Cover and cook at a simmer for 1 hour.

7. Remove the cover. Allow to come back to a boil. Lower the heat to medium. Add in the chopped Yukon gold potatoes and chopped carrots. Continue to cook for 45 minutes or until the vegetables are soft.
8. Toss out the bay leaves.
9. Remove from heat.
10. Serve immediately.

(8) Cuban Beef Stew

This is another delicious beef stew recipe you can make whenever you are craving authentic Spanish cuisine. It is unlike any other beef stew recipe you have ever tried before.

Yield: 4 servings

Cooking Time: 4 hours and 25 minutes

List of Ingredients:

- 1 ½ pounds of beef stew meat, cut into ½ inch sized cubes
- 1 green bell pepper, sliced
- 1 red bell pepper, sliced
- 1 yellow bell pepper, sliced
- 1 bulb of garlic, peeled and minced
- 1, 18 ounce can of tomatoes, crushed
- Dash of salt and black pepper
- ½ teaspoons of powdered cumin
- ½ teaspoons of dried oregano
- ½ teaspoons of smoked paprika
- 1 tablespoon of canola oil

MMMMMMMMMMMMMMMMMMMMMMMMMMMMMMMMMMMMM

Methods:

1. In a pot set over medium to high heat, add in the canola oil. Add in the beef cubes. Cook for 5 minutes or until browned. Transfer into a bowl of a slow cooker.

2. Add in the powdered cumin, dried oregano and smoked paprika. Season with a dash of salt and black pepper.

3. In the pot, add in the sliced red, green and yellow bell peppers. Stir well to mix. Cook for 5 minutes or until soft. Transfer into the slow cooker. Add the minced garlic over the top.

4. Pour in the crushed tomatoes into the slow cooker.

5. Cover and cook on the highest setting for 4 hours.

6. Remove the cover and serve immediately.

(9) Classic Homemade Beef Stew

Homemade beef stew is the best comfort food to enjoy on any cold or rainy day. This dish is no different and makes for a perfect meal the entire family will love.

Yield: 8 servings

Cooking Time: 1 hour and 35 minutes

List of Ingredients:

- 1/3 cup of all-purpose flour
- 1 teaspoon of sea salt
- ½ teaspoons of black pepper
- ½ teaspoons of powdered onion
- ½ teaspoons of Italian seasoning
- 1 ½ to 2 pounds of beef chuck roast, cut into small cubes
- Vegetable oil, as needed and evenly divided
- 1 onion, chopped
- 4 cloves of garlic, minced
- 1 to 2 Tablespoons of red wine
- 6 Tablespoons of tomato paste
- 3 Russet potatoes, peeled and chopped into small cubes
- 1 sweet potato, peeled and chopped into small cubes
- 2 carrots, peeled and chopped
- 2 stalks of celery, chopped
- ½ a star anise
- 1 to 2 teaspoons of Worcestershire sauce
- 2 teaspoons of Italian seasoning

- 1 bay leaf
- 4 cups of beef broth
- Water, as needed
- 2 teaspoons of cornstarch + 3 teaspoons of water
- 2 Tablespoons of parsley, chopped and for garnish
- Dash of salt and black pepper

MMMMMMMMMMMMMMMMMMMMMMMMMMMMMMMMMMMMMM

Methods:

1. In a Ziploc bag, add in the all-purpose flour, dash of sea salt, dash of black pepper, powdered onion and Italian seasoning. Stir gently to mix. Add in the beef chuck roast cubes and seal the bag. Toss well to coat.

2. In a Dutch oven set over medium to high heat, add in 1 to 2 tablespoons of vegetable oil. Add in the coated meat. Cook for 2 to 3 minutes or until seared on all sides. Transfer onto a plate and set aside.

3. Add 1 tablespoon of vegetable oil. Add in the chopped onions and minced garlic. Cook for 1 minute or until the onions are soft. Add in the red wine and deglaze the bottom of the Dutch oven. Add in the tomato paste and continue to cook for 2 minutes.

4. Add the beef back into the Dutch oven. Add in the chopped potatoes, chopped sweet potato, chopped carrots, chopped celery, start anise, remaining Italian seasoning, Worcestershire sauce, beef broth and bay leaf. Stir gently to mix.

5. Allow to come to a boil. Lower the heat to low and cover. Cook for 2 hours or until the potatoes and beef are soft.

6. In a bowl, add in the cornstarch and water. Whisk to mix. Add into the stew and stir well to incorporate. Allow to come back to a boil over high heat. Cook for 1 to 2 minutes or until thick in consistency.

7. Season with a dash of salt and black pepper.

8. Serve with a garnish of chopped parsley.

(10) Slow Cooker Beef Tip Stew with Rice

This is the perfect beef stew dish for you to make during the week. It is made in a slow cooker, so you don't have to put much effort into making this dish.

Yield: 6 servings

Cooking Time: 8 hours and 10 minutes

List of Ingredients:

- 2 pounds of beef stew meat, cut into 1 inch sized cubes
- 1, 10.75 ounce can of cream of mushroom soup
- 1, 1.61 ounce pack of brown gravy mix
- 1 beef bouillon cube
- 1 cup of water
- 1 onion, chopped
- White rice, cooked and for serving

MMMMMMMMMMMMMMMMMMMMMMMMMMMMMMMMMMMMM

Methods:

1. In the bowl of a slow cooker, add in all of the ingredients. Stir gently to mix.
2. Cover and cook on the lowest setting for 7 to 8 hours.
3. Serve over the cooked white rice immediately.

(11)   Irish Coffee Beef Stew

If you never thought coffee would make a delicious addition to a classic beef stew dish, you will be pleasantly surprised once you try this dish for yourself.

Yield: 6 servings

Cooking Time: 3 hours and 10 minutes

List of Ingredients:

- 2 ½ Tablespoons of extra virgin olive oil
- 2 ½ pounds of beef chuck, boneless
- Dash of salt and black pepper
- 4 cloves of garlic, minced
- 7 slices of bacon, chopped
- 3 ½ Tablespoons of all-purpose flour
- 1, 14.9 ounce can of Guinness beer
- 5 Tablespoons of tomato paste
- 3 cups of chicken stock
- 4 carrots, peeled and cut into thin slices
- 2 stalks of celery, cut into 1 inch sized pieces
- 1 parsnip, peeled and cut into ½ inch sized pieces
- 2 bay leaves
- 1 teaspoon of dried thyme
- 1 teaspoon of pure coffee extract
- ¼ cup of water
- 3 dried prunes, chopped
- 8 red potatoes, cut into quarters

MMMMMMMMMMMMMMMMMMMMMMMMMMMMMMMMMMMMM

Methods:

1. In a bowl, season the beef chuck with a dash of salt and black pepper.

2. In a Dutch oven set over high heat, add in the olive oil. Add in the seasoned beef cubes. Cook for 2 to 3 minutes or until browned. Transfer onto a plate and set aside.

3. Lower the heat to medium. Add in the chopped onions and minced garlic. Season with a dash of salt. Cook for 5 minutes or until soft.

4. Add in the bacon pieces. Continue to cook for 5 minutes or until crispy.

5. Add in the all-purpose flour. Whisk well until smooth in consistency. Cook for an additional minute.

6. Add in the can of Guinness beer and deglaze the bottom of the Dutch oven. Add in the tomato paste, chicken stock, carrot slices, chopped celery, chopped parsnip pieces, bay leaves, dried thyme, water and pure coffee extract. Stir well until incorporated.

7. Add in the cooked beef and allow to come to a boil. Lower the heat to low. Cover and cook for 2 hours or until the beef is soft.

8. Remove the cover. Add in the chopped red potato quarters and chopped prunes. Continue to cook for an additional 30 to 40 minutes or until the sauce is thick in consistency.

9. Season with a dash of salt and black pepper. Remove the bay leaves.

10. Remove from heat and serve immediately.

(12) Wild Mushroom Beef Stew

This is an elegant beef stew that can be made for practically any occasion. Made with wild mushrooms and plenty of fresh herbs, this is an elegant beef stew that everybody will fall in love with.

Yield: 6 servings

Cooking Time: 2 hours

List of Ingredients:

- 2 pounds of beef chuck roast, cut into 1 inch cubes
- 1 onion, chopped
- 1 pound of wild mushrooms, chopped
- 1 bay leaf
- 5 cloves of garlic, minced
- 6 sprigs of thyme
- 1 cup of Cognac
- Vegetable oil, as needed
- Dash of salt and black pepper
- 2 quarts of beef stock

MMMMMMMMMMMMMMMMMMMMMMMMMMMMMMMMMMMM

Methods:

1. Season the beef chuck roast cubes with a dash of salt and black pepper.
2. In a Dutch oven set over medium to high heat, add in 2 tablespoons of vegetable oil.
3. Preheat the oven to 325 degrees.
4. Add the seasoned beef cubes into the pot. Cook for 2 to 3 minutes or until browned on all sides. Transfer into a bowl and set aside.
5. In the pot, add in the chopped onions, minced garlic, bay leaf and chopped mushrooms. Cook for 10 minutes or until soft.
6. Add the cooked beef cubes back into the pot. Sprinkle with a dash of all-purpose flour. Toss until coated.
7. Pour in the Cognac. Deglaze the bottom of the pot. Cook for 3 minutes or until the alcohol has been cooked out. Add in the beef stock to cover.
8. Transfer into the oven to bake for 30 minutes. Lower the temperature of the oven to 275 degrees. Continue to cook for an hour and 15 minutes or until the beef is soft.
9. Remove and serve immediately.

(13) Slow Cooker Beef Bourguignon Stew

This is a delicious beef stew recipe that is made with crazy tender beef that will melt in your mouth with every bite.

Yield: 6 servings

Cooking Time: 9 hours and 20 minutes

List of Ingredients:

- 5 slices of bacon, chopped
- 3 pounds of beef chuck, cut into small cubes
- 1 cup of dried red wine
- 2 cups of chicken broth
- ½ cup of tomato sauce
- ¼ cup of soy sauce
- ¼ cup of all-purpose flour
- 3 cloves of garlic, chopped
- 2 Tablespoons of thyme, chopped
- 5 carrots, thinly sliced
- 1 pound of baby potatoes
- 8 ounces of mushrooms, thinly sliced
- Parsley, chopped and for garnish

MMMMMMMMMMMMMMMMMMMMMMMMMMMMMMMMMMMMM

Methods:

1. In a skillet set over medium to high heat, add in the bacon. Cook for 5 minutes or until crispy. Transfer into a slow cooker.

2. Season the beef cubes with a dash of salt and black pepper. Add into the skillet. Cook for 2 to 3 minutes or until seared on all sides. Transfer into the slow cooker.

3. Add the dried red wine into the skillet. Deglaze the bottom of the skillet. Allow to come to a simmer.

4. Add in the chicken broth, tomato sauce and soy sauce. Allow to come to a simmer. Add in the all-purpose flour. Whisk until smooth in consistency. Pour into the slow cooker.

5. Add in the chopped garlic, chopped thyme, sliced carrots, baby potatoes and sliced mushrooms. Stir gently to mix.

6. Cover and cook on the lowest setting for 8 to 10 hours or on the highest setting for 6 to 8 hours.

7. Serve with a garnish of chopped parsley.

(14) Mexican Beef Stew

Make this delicious beef stew recipe whenever you are craving a meal with an exotic Latin flavor. One bite and I guarantee you will become hooked.

Yield: 8 to 10 servings

Cooking Time: 8 hours and 15 minutes

List of Ingredients:

- 2 ½ pounds of beef stew meat, cut into 1 inch cubes
- 4 teaspoons of vegetable oil
- 1 teaspoon of salt
- 1 teaspoon of black pepper
- 1 white onion, peeled and chopped
- 1 red bell pepper, seeds removed and chopped
- 1 jalapeno peppers, seeds removed and chopped
- 5 cloves of garlic, minced
- 1 ½ teaspoons of powdered cumin
- ¾ teaspoons of powdered chili
- ¾ teaspoons of dried oregano
- 4 Tablespoons of all-purpose flour
- 1 ¾ cup of low sodium chicken broth
- 2 tomatoes, chopped
- 2 bay leaves

Ingredients for serving:

- 1 pack of flour tortillas
- 1 cup of queso cotija, crumbled
- ½ cup of cilantro, chopped
- 3 stalks of green onions, thinly sliced

MMMMMMMMMMMMMMMMMMMMMMMMMMMMMMMMMMMMMM

Methods:

1. In a skillet set over medium to high heat, add in 2 teaspoons of vegetable oil. Add in the beef cubes. Season with a dash of salt and black pepper. Cook for 5 minutes or until browned. Transfer into a slow cooker.

2. In the same skillet, add in 2 teaspoons of vegetable oil. Add in the chopped onion, chopped red bell pepper, chopped jalapeno pepper and minced garlic. Cook for 5 minutes or until soft.

3. Add in the powdered cumin, powdered chili, dried oregano and all-purpose flour. Stir well to mix. Cook for an additional minute.

4. Slowly add in the low sodium chicken broth. Deglaze the bottom of the skillet. Cook at a simmer for 2 minutes. Transfer into a slow cooker. Season with a dash of salt and black pepper.

5. Cover and cook on the lowest setting for 8 to 10 hours.

6. Remove the cover.

7. Serve immediately on the flour tortillas. Top off with the crumbled queso, chopped cilantro and sliced green onions.

(15) Beef Stew Pot Pie

If you are looking for something extra filling, then this is the perfect beef stew dish that you can make. While it may take some effort to prepare, it is well worth the effort in the end.

Yield: 6 servings

Cooking Time: 2 hours and 30 minutes

List of Ingredients:

- 2 pounds of beef chuck roast, cut into ½ inch thick cubes
- 1 onion, chopped
- 4 cloves of garlic, minced
- 3 sticks of celery, chopped
- 10 to 12 mushrooms, thinly sliced
- 2 cups of potatoes, chopped
- 1 ½ ups of peas and carrots, mixed
- 2 Tablespoons of tomato paste
- 1 teaspoon of dried thyme
- ½ teaspoons of dried rosemary
- 1 bay leaf
- 1 ½ cups of Guinness beer
- 2 cups of beef broth
- 3 Tablespoons of light brown sugar
- 2 Tablespoons of flour + 1 tablespoon of water, mixed together
- Dash of salt and black pepper
- 2 to 3 Tablespoons of extra virgin olive oil
- 1 handful of parsley, chopped
- 1 pack of puff pastry
- 1 egg + 1 tablespoon of water, beaten together

Methods:

1. Season the beef chuck roast cubes with a dash of salt and black pepper.

2. In a Dutch oven set over medium to high heat, add in 2 tablespoons of extra virgin olive oil. Add in the beef cubes. Cook for 2 to 3 minutes or until browned. Remove and transfer into a bowl.

3. Add in the chopped onions. Cook for 5 minutes or until soft. Add in the minced garlic. Cook for an additional minute.

4. Add in the chopped celery and sliced mushrooms. Cook for 5 minutes or until soft.

5. Add in the tomato paste, dried thyme and dried rosemary. Stir well to mix. Season with a dash of salt. Add the cooked beef back into the Dutch oven. Add in the light brown sugar and bay leave. Lower the heat to low.

6. Cover and cook at a simmer for 1 hour.

7. Add in the chopped potatoes. Allow to come back to a boil. Cook for 15 to 20 minutes or until the potatoes are soft.

8. Add in the flour and water mix. Stir well to incorporate. Allow to come back to a boil. Cook for 2 to 3 minutes or until thick in consistency.

9. Remove from heat. Add in the carrot mix and chopped parsley. Stir well to incorporate. 10. Preheat the oven to 400 degrees.

10. Roll out the puff pastry to fit a pie plate. Place into a grease pie plate. Trim the edges. Roll out the second puff pastry to cover the top. Pour the beef stew filling into the crust. Cover with the top puff pastry and crimp the edges to seal.

11. Brush the top with the egg wash.

12. Place into the oven to bake for 25 to 30 minutes or until golden.

13. Remove and rest for 20 minutes. 15. Serve.

(16) Guinness Beef Stew with Cheddar Herb Dumplings

If you want to spoil your friends and family with something extra special, then this is the perfect beef stew dish for you to make.

Yield: 8 servings

Cooking Time: 2 hours and 10 minutes

Ingredients for the stew:

- 2 pounds of beef chuck roast, cut into 1 inch sized cubes
- ¼ pound of applewood smoked bacon
- 1 onion, chopped
- 1 stalk of celery, chopped
- 2 carrots, peeled and chopped
- 2 cloves of garlic, thinly sliced
- 2 turnips, peeled and chopped
- 2 parsnips, chopped
- 4 ounces of tomato paste
- 12 ounces of Guinness stout
- 4 cups of low sodium beef broth
- 1 bay leaf
- 3 sprigs of thyme
- Parsley, chopped
- ½ pound of cremini mushrooms, thinly sliced

Ingredients for the dumplings:

- 1 ½ cups of self-rising flour
- ½ teaspoons of powdered garlic
- ¼ cup of shortening
- ½ cup of sharp cheddar cheese, shredded
- 2/3 cup of whole milk
- 1 to 2 Tablespoons of mixed herbs, chopped

MMMMMMMMMMMMMMMMMMMMMMMMMMMMMMMMMMMMMM

Methods:

1. In a pot set over medium heat, add in the applewood smoked bacon. Cook for 5 minutes or until crispy. Transfer onto a plate lined with paper towels to drain.

2. Season the beef chuck roast cubes with a dash of salt and black pepper. Add into the pot. Cook for 2 to 3 minutes or until seared on all sides. Transfer into a bowl and set aside.

3. In the same pot, add in the chopped onion, chopped celery and chopped carrots. Cook for 5 minutes or until soft. Add in the minced garlic. Cook for an additional minute.

4. Add in the tomato paste. Stir well to mix.

5. Add in the Guinness stout and Worcestershire sauce. Allow to come to a simmer. Deglaze the bottom of the pot. Add in the cooked beef, beef stock, bay leaf and sprigs of thyme. Stir gently to incorporate.

6. Lower the heat to low. Cover and cook for 1 hour and 30 minutes. Add in the chopped carrots, chopped parsnips and turnips. Continue to cook for an additional 30 minutes or until the vegetables are soft. Remove the bay leaf and thyme sprigs.

7. Add in the sliced mushrooms. Cook for an additional 10 minutes.

8. In a bowl, add in the self-rising flour and powdered garlic. Stir well to mix. Add in the shortening and cut in with a pastry cutter until crumbly in consistency. Add in the shredded cheddar cheese and milk. Stir well until moist.

9. Shape the dough into small balls. Gently add them into the stew.

10. Cover and continue to cook for 25 minutes over low heat or until firm.

11. Remove from heat.

12. Serve immediately with a garnish of chopped parsley.

(17) Instant Pot Beef Stew

The Instant pot is the perfect cooking tool to use whenever you want to put as little effort into preparing dinner for the entire family. This dish is no different and can be made in just a few hours.

Yield: 5 servings

Cooking Time: 1 hour and 20 minutes

List of Ingredients:

- 1 ½ pounds of beef chuck roast, cut into ½ inch sized cubes
- 1, 16 ounce bag of pearl onions
- 8 ounces of carrots, peeled and chopped into 1 inch sized pieces
- 1 Russet potatoes, peeled and cut into 1 inch sized cubes
- 10 ounces of mushrooms, sliced into quarters
- 2 cups of beef stock
- 3 Tablespoons of tomato paste
- 3 Tablespoons of all-purpose flour
- 1 tablespoon of butter
- 1 teaspoon of salt

MMMMMMMMMMMMMMMMMMMMMMMMMMMMMMMMMM

Methods:

1. In a bowl, add in the beef chuck roast cubes and all-purpose flour. Toss well to coat.

2. In a pressure cooker, add in the butter. Set to the medium setting. Once the butter melts, add in the coated beef cubes. Cook for 5 minutes or until browned on all sides.

3. Add the beef broth into the instant pot. Deglaze the bottom of the instant pot. Add in the tomato paste. Season with a dash of salt.

4. Add in the remaining ingredients. Stir well to incorporate.

5. Cover and lock the pressure cooker. Set to the stew setting and cook for 35 minutes. Once finished, allow to rest for 10 minutes before releasing the lid.

6. Stir well to mix.

7. Season with a dash of salt and black pepper.

8. Serve immediately with a garnish of chopped parsley.

(18) Beef Stew Shepherd's Pie

This is a grown-up version of a classic Shepherd's pie that every adult in your household won't be able to help but fall in love with.

Yield: 6 servings

Cooking Time: 50 minutes

Ingredients for the stew:

- 1 pound of beef stew meat, cut into cubes
- Chicken stock, as needed
- 1 tablespoon of butter
- 1 tablespoon of all-purpose flour

Ingredients for the potatoes:

- 1 pound of Russet potatoes, peeled and cut into cubes
- 3/8 cup of warm milk
- 1 tablespoon of butter
- 1 egg yolk
- 4 ounces of gruyere cheese, grated
- Dash of salt

MMMMMMMMMMMMMMMMMMMMMMMMMMMMMMMMMMM

Methods:

1. Preheat the oven to 350 degrees.
2. In a pot set over medium to high heat, fill with water. Add in the potato cubes. Allow to come to a boil. Cook for 30 minutes or until the potatoes are soft. Drain and set aside.
3. In a saucepan set over medium heat, add in 4 cups of chicken stock. Allow to come to a boil. Add in the beef cubes and allow to simmer for a few minutes.
4. In a bowl, add in the butter and all-purpose flour. Stir well until crumbly in consistency. Add into the chicken broth mix and stir well to incorporate.
5. In a separate bowl, add in the drained Russet potatoes, warm milk and 1 tablespoon of butter. Mash well until smooth in consistency. Add in the egg yolk and grated gruyere cheese. Stir well until evenly mixed.
6. Pour the stew into a baking dish. Spread the mashed potatoes over the top.
7. Place into the oven to bake for 20 minutes.
8. Increase the temperature of the oven to a broil. Broil for 5 minutes or until browned on the top.
9. Remove and set aside to rest for 15 minutes.
10. Slice and serve.

(19) French Beef Stew

This is a delicious beef stew recipe you can make whenever you want to make something elegant to impress your friends and family.

Yield: 8 servings

Cooking Time: 2 to 3 hours and 25 minutes

List of Ingredients:

- 3 pounds of beef stew, cut into 1 inch sized cubes
- 1, 750 ml bottle of dried red wine
- Dash of salt and black pepper
- 3 sprigs of thyme
- 2 bay leaves
- 3 carrots, peeled and thinly sliced
- 1 orange, sliced into 8 wedges
- 1 onion, peeled and sliced into rings
- 2 cloves of garlic, peeled and thinly sliced
- Extra virgin olive oil, as needed
- 1, 6 ounce can of tomato paste
- 3 ½ ounces of black olives, pits removed

MMMMMMMMMMMMMMMMMMMMMMMMMMMMMMMMMMMM

Methods:

1. Season the beef cubes with a dash of salt and black pepper. Transfer into a bowl.
2. In the bowl, add in the dried red wine, thyme sprigs, bay leaves, sliced carrots, orange wedges, sliced onion rings and sliced garlic. Stir well to mix.
3. Cover and set into the fridge to marinate for 12 hours.
4. In a stockpot set over medium heat, add in the olive oil. Add the beef cubes and cook for 5 minutes or until browned on all sides.
5. Pour the marinade into the stockpot. Allow to come to a boil. Cook for 5 minutes. Lower the heat to low. Add in the tomato paste and 4 ½ cups of water. Cover and allow to simmer over low heat for 2 to 3 hours.
6. Add in the black olives. Continue to cook for 15 minutes.
7. Remove from heat and serve immediately.

(20) Irish Beef Stew

This is a delicious beef stew that is made with plenty of beef, Guinness beer and potatoes to make a filling dish the entire family will love.

Yield: 4 to 6 servings

Cooking Time: 2 hours and 20 minutes

List of Ingredients:

- 1 ¼ pounds of beef chuck meat, cut into 1 ½ inch cubes
- 3 teaspoons of salt
- ¼ cup of extra virgin olive oil
- 6 cloves of garlic, minced
- 4 cups of beef stock
- 2 cups of water
- 1 cup of Guinness stout
- 1 cup of dried red wine
- 2 Tablespoons of tomato paste
- 1 tablespoon of white sugar
- 1 teaspoon of dried thyme
- 1 tablespoon of Worcestershire sauce
- 2 bay leaves
- 2 Tablespoons of butter
- 3 pounds of russet potatoes, peeled and cut into ½ inch sized pieces
- 1 onion, chopped
- 2 cups of carrots, peeled and cut into ½ inch sized pieces

- ½ teaspoons of black pepper
- 2 Tablespoons of parsley, chopped

MMMMMMMMMMMMMMMMMMMMMMMMMMMMMMMMMMMM

Methods:

1. Season the beef chuck pieces with a dash of salt and black pepper.

2. In a pot set over medium to high heat, add in the olive oil. Add in the beef pieces. Cook for 2 to 3 minutes or until seared on all sides. Transfer into a bowl and set aside.

3. In the pot, add in the minced garlic. Cook for 1 minute. Add in the Guinness stout, beet stock, water, dried red wine, tomato paste, white sugar, dried thyme, Worcestershire sauce and bay leaves. Stir well to mix.

4. Allow to come to a simmer. Lower the heat to low. Cover and continue to simmer for 1 hour.

5. In a separate pot set over medium heat, add in the butter. Add in the chopped onions and chopped carrots. Cook for 15 minutes or until golden. Transfer into a pot with the broth.

6. Season with a dash of salt and black pepper.

7. Cover and simmer for 40 minutes or until soft.

8. Toss out the bay leaves.

9. Remove from heat. Season with an additional dash of salt and black pepper.

10. Serve immediately with a garnish of chopped parsley.

(21) Beef Stew Burgundy

This is a classic and hearty beef stew recipe you can make whenever you want to spoil your significant other with something special.

Yield: 6 to 8 servings

Cooking Time: 8 hours and 15 minutes

List of Ingredients:

- 2.2 pounds of beef chuck roast, cut into 1 inch sized cubes
- 1 tablespoon of extra virgin olive oil
- 4 strips of bacon, chopped
- 2 onions, chopped
- 3 cloves of garlic, peeled and crushed
- 1 ½ cups of carrots, thinly sliced
- 1 ½ cups of red potatoes, thinly sliced
- 1 bouquet garni
- 1 1/3 cup of dried red wine
- 8 ounces of mushrooms, chopped
- Dash of salt and black pepper

MMMMMMMMMMMMMMMMMMMMMMMMMMMMMMMMMMM

Methods:

1. Season the beef cubes with a dash of salt and black pepper.

2. In a Dutch oven set over medium to high heat, add in the olive oil. Add in the chopped bacon. Cook for 5 minutes or until crispy. Transfer onto a plate lined with paper towels to drain.

3. In the Dutch oven, add in the beef cubes. Cook for 2 to 3 minutes or until the beef is browned. Transfer into a bowl and set aside.

4. Add in the chopped onions and crushed garlic. Cook for 5 minutes or until soft. Transfer into a slow cooker along with the beef cubes and chopped bacon.

5. In the slow cooker, add in the sliced carrots, sliced red potatoes, garni, dried red wine and chopped mushrooms. Season with a dash of salt and black pepper.

6. Cover and cook on the lowest setting for 6 to 8 hours.

7. Serve immediately.

(22) Fall Beef Stew

Just as the name implies, this is the perfect stew recipe to make just in time for when the weather begins to turn cold.

Yield: 6 servings

Cooking Time: 3 hours and 20 minutes

List of Ingredients:

- 3 Tablespoons of extra virgin olive oil
- 2 Tablespoons of butter
- 3 pounds of chuck roast, cut into 1 inch sized cubes
- 1 onion, chopped
- 3 cloves of garlic minced
- 1/3 cup of all-purpose flour
- 1/3 cup of Italian parsley, chopped
- 6 sprigs of thyme
- 3 bay leaves
- 4 cloves, whole
- Dash of sea salt
- Dash of black pepper
- 1 tablespoon of smoked paprika
- Dash of crushed red pepper flakes
- 1 ¼ quarts of water, filtered
- 3/5 cup of green peas
- 1 cup of cherry tomatoes, chopped
- ¾ pound of golden potatoes, chopped into cubes
- 2 carrots, thinly sliced

MMMMMMMMMMMMMMMMMMMMMMMMMMMMMMMMMMM

Methods:

1. In a Dutch oven set over medium heat, add in 2 tablespoons of olive oil. Season the beef chuck cubes with a dash of sea salt and black pepper. Add into the Dutch oven. Cook for 2 to 3 minutes or until seared on all sides Transfer into a bowl and set aside.

2. Add in 2 tablespoons of butter and 1 tablespoon of olive oil into the Dutch oven. Add in the chopped onions. Cook for 5 minutes or until soft. Add in the minced garlic and dash of crushed red pepper flakes. Cook for an additional minute.

3. Add in the all-purpose flour and smoked paprika. Cook for an additional minute.

4. Add in the water and deglaze the bottom of the Dutch oven. Allow to come to a simmer. Add in the seared beef cubes, bay leaf, whole cloves and sprigs of thyme. Cover and lower the heat to low. Cook for 2 ½ hours or until the beef cubes are soft.

5. Add in the golden potato cubes and sliced carrots. Cover and continue to cook for an additional 20 minutes or until the potatoes are soft. Remove from heat.

6. Add in the tomatoes and peas. Stir well to incorporate. Cover and set aside to rest for 20 minutes.
7. Season with a dash of salt and black pepper.
8. Serve with a garnish of chopped parsley.

(23) Old Fashioned Beef Stew

This is a delicious beef stew recipe whenever you have a craving for your grandparents' cooking. It is so delicious, I know you will want to make it as often as possible.

Yield: 4 servings

Cooking Time: 2 hours and 45 minutes

List of Ingredients:

- 3 teaspoons of extra virgin olive oil, evenly divided
- 1 pound of beef meat, fat trimmed
- 1 cup of onion, chopped
- 1 clove of garlic, minced
- 2 ½ cups of beef stock
- ½ teaspoons of salt
- ½ teaspoons of dried thyme leaves
- 1 bay leaf
- 4 red potatoes, cut into 1 inch sized cubes
- 2 carrots, thinly sliced
- 2 stalks of celery, thinly sliced
- 2 ½ Tablespoons of all-purpose flour
- ¼ cup of beef stock

MMMMMMMMMMMMMMMMMMMMMMMMMMMMMMMMMMMMMM

Methods:

1. In a Dutch oven set over medium to high heat, add in 2 teaspoons of olive oil. Add in the beef cubes. Season with a dash of salt and black pepper. Cook for 5 minute or until browned on all sides.

2. Add in an additional teaspoon of olive oil. Add in the chopped onion and minced garlic. Cook for 5 minutes or until soft.

3. Add in the beef stock, dash of salt, dried thyme leaves and bay leaf. Stir gently to mix. Allow to come to a boil. Lower the heat to low. Cover and cook for 2 hours or until the beef is soft.

4. Add in the potato cubes, sliced carrots and sliced celery. Stir well to incorporate. Allow to come back to a boil. Cover and continue to cook for 15 minutes or until the vegetables are soft.

5. In a bowl, add in ¼ cup of beef stock and the all-purpose flour. Whisk until smooth in consistency. Pour into the stew. Continue to cook for 5 minutes or until thick in consistency. 6. Remove from heat and serve immediately.

(24) Chunky Beef Stew

This is a chunky and savory beef stew that can be made to satisfy all of those picky eaters in your home. Since it is made in a slow cooker, no beef stew is as easy to make as this dish.

Yield: 6 servings

Cooking Time: 8 to 10 hours

List of Ingredients:

- 1 pound of lean chuck beef, cut into cubes
- ¼ cup of all-purpose flour
- 2 Tablespoons of extra virgin olive oil
- 2 stalks of celery, thinly sliced
- 3 carrots, sliced into rounds
- ½ cup of snap peas, shelled
- 2 potatoes, peeled and cut into pieces
- ½ cup of red bell pepper, chopped
- 1 yellow onion, chopped
- 2 cloves of garlic, minced
- 1 bay leaf
- 2 teaspoons of dried thyme
- 1 teaspoon of salt
- Dash of black pepper
- 2 ½ cups of low sodium beef broth
- ½ cup of beef broth
- ¼ cup of parsley, chopped
- 2 Tablespoons of tomato paste

MMMMMMMMMMMMMMMMMMMMMMMMMMMMMMMMMM

Methods:

1. In a bowl, add in the lean chuck beef cubes and all-purpose flour. Toss well until coated.

2. In a skillet set over medium to high heat, add in the olive oil and coated beef. Cook for 2 to 3 minutes on each side or until seared. Transfer into a slow cooker.

3. Add in the remaining ingredients except for the chopped parsley. Stir well to mix.

4. Cover and cook on the lowest setting for 8 to 10 hours or until the beef is soft.

5. Remove the bay leaf.

6. Serve immediately with a garnish of chopped parsley.

(25) Hearty Beef Stew

This is a perfect beef stew you can make whenever you are craving warm comfort food. Made with hearty dumplings, this is a dish that will please all who try it.

Yield: 8 servings

Cooking Time: 3 hours and 30 minutes

List of Ingredients:

- 2 pounds of beef chuck roast, cut into cubes
- 3 Tablespoons of all-purpose flour
- Dash of salt and black pepper
- 2 Tablespoons of vegetable oil
- 2 Tablespoons of butter
- 5 carrots, peeled and cut into cubes
- 3 pounds of yellow potatoes, peeled and cut into cubes
- 1 onion, chopped
- 5 cloves of garlic, minced
- ¼ cup of all-purpose flour
- 1 teaspoon of dried oregano
- 2 bay leaves
- 3 cups of beef broth
- 2 cups of water
- ½ cup of peas
- Dash of salt and black pepper

MMMMMMMMMMMMMMMMMMMMMMMMMMMMMMMMMMM

Methods:

1. In a stock pot set over medium to high heat, add in the vegetable oil.

2. In a bowl, add in 2 tablespoons of all-purpose flour, dash of salt and black pepper. Add in the beef chuck cubes. Toss well until coated.

3. In the stockpot, add in the coated beef. Cook for 2 minutes on each side or until seared. Remove and transfer the beef cubes into a bowl.

4. Add the butter into the stockpot. Lower the heat to medium. Add in the carrot cubes, yellow potato cubes and chopped onion. Cook for 6 to 8 minutes or until soft. Add in the minced garlic. Cook for 1 minute. Add in ¼ cup of all-purpose flour. Whisk until smooth in consistency.

5. Continue to cook for 1 minute. Add in 1 cup of the beef broth. Stir well to mix. Add in the cooked beef and the remaining beef broth. Add in the water and bay leaves. Increase the temperature to a high medium. Allow to come to a boil. Cook for 2 minutes. Lower the heat to low. Cover and cook for 2 hours or until the beef is soft.

6. Add in the peas. Continue to cook for 30 minutes or until the peas are cooked through.

7. Season with a dash of salt and black pepper.

8. Remove the bay leaves.

9. Remove from heat and serve immediately.

About the Author

A native of Indianapolis, Indiana, Valeria Ray found her passion for cooking while she was studying English Literature at Oakland City University. She decided to try a cooking course with her friends and the experience changed her forever. She enrolled at the Art Institute of Indiana which offered extensive courses in the culinary Arts. Once Ray dipped her toe in the cooking world, she never looked back.

When Valeria graduated, she worked in French restaurants in the Indianapolis area until she became the head chef at one of the 5-star establishments in the area. Valeria's attention to taste and visual detail caught the eye of a local business person who expressed an interest in publishing her recipes. Valeria began her secondary career authoring cookbooks and e-books which she tackled with as much talent and gusto as her first career. Her passion for food leaps off the page of her books which have colourful anecdotes and stunning pictures of dishes she has prepared herself.

Valeria Ray lives in Indianapolis with her husband of 15 years, Tom, her daughter, Isobel and their loveable Golden Retriever, Goldy. Valeria enjoys cooking special dishes in her large, comfortable kitchen where the family gets involved in preparing meals. This successful, dynamic chef is an inspiration to culinary students and novice cooks everywhere.

••••••••• ● ● ● ● ● ●•••••••

Author's Afterthoughts

Thank you for Purchasing my book and taking the time to read it from front to back. I am always grateful when a reader chooses my work and I hope you enjoyed it!

With the vast selection available online, I am touched that you chose to be purchasing my work and take valuable time out of your life to read it. My hope is that you feel you made the right decision.

I very much would like to know what you thought of the book. Please take the time to write an honest and informative review on Amazon.com. Your experience and opinions will be of great benefit to me and those readers looking to make an informed choice.

With much thanks,

Valeria Ray